BORROWED LIGHT

BORROWED LIGHT

Shirley Robertson

ACKNOWLEDGEMENTS:

My husband, George B. Robertson, for his patience, support and interest.

Sherman Hines, MPA, for his generous approach in sharing knowledge through his teaching "The Art of Seeing Light".

©
Stonehurst Publishing Company
Halifax, Nova Scotia
ISBN-0-9691923-0-4

Printed and bound in Hong Kong by
The Everbest Printing Company Limited

Distributed by
Nimbus Publishing Limited
P.O. Box 9321, Station A
Halifax, Nova Scotia
Canada
B3K 5N5

Photographs taken with Pentax 35mm.

In loving memory of Gladys and Fred Barnstead
— my mother and father.

If you are burdened with a load of care
And would some surcease from your burden find,
Come walk with me in shady places, where
The peace and quiet soothe a troubled mind.

— Howard Murray Whitman

Shirley Robertson's remarkable photographs reveal
to us much of the beauty and mystery around us, which we often
pass by unnoticed — a seagull soaring above the sullen sea; a drop of
water on a leaf or branch, or the intricate design of a fungus or lichen.

Her natural and emotional approach accomplishes this
most skillfully and, of special interest, is her use of a narrowed depth
of focus to concentrate our attention on a particular part of her
subject without entirely isolating it from its surroundings.
She makes it easy and enjoyable for us to see what we sometimes
look at without really seeing and enjoying.

— Henry D. Hicks, C.C., Q.C.

And God said, "Let there be light",
and there was light.

— Genesis, 1:3

Feel yourself, and be not daunted by things

— Emerson

The clouds are passing far and high;
We little birds in them play.
And everything that can sing and fly
Goes with us, and far away.

— Longfellow

Oh, could I flow like thee, and make thy stream
My great example, as it is my theme!
Though deep yet clear, though gentle yet not dull,
Strong without rage, without o'er flowing full.

— Sir John Denham

Yellow buttercups stud the green carpet
like golden buttons.

— Longfellow

Life is a series of surprises,
and would not be worth taking
or keeping if it were not.

— Emerson

I go to prove my soul!
I see my way as birds their trackless way.

— Browning

Thy leaf has perished in the green,
And while we breathe beneath the sun,
The world which credits what is done
Is cold to all that might have been.

— Tennyson

Nature tells every secret once.

— Emerson

Nature never becomes a toy to a wise spirit.

— Emerson

The little reed, bending to the force of the wind,
soon stood upright again when the storm had passed over.

— Aesop

The sun is a special body
possessed of the power to
communicate itself to all things;
this power is light.

— Johannes Kepler

How often, oh, how often
I had wished that the ebbing tide
Would bear me away on its bosom
O'er the ocean wild and wide!

— Emerson

He giveth snow like wool;
He scattereth the hoar like ashes.

— Psalm 147:16

Ye living flowers that skirt the eternal frost.

— Coleridge

How much of human life is lost in waiting!
Tomorrow will be like today.
Life wastes itself while we are preparing to live.

— Emerson

When I am dead, my dearest,
Sing no sad songs for me;
Plant thou no roses at my head,
Nor shady cypress tree.
Be the green grass above me
With showers and dewdrops wet;
And if thou wilt, remember
And if thou wilt, forget.

— Christina Rossetti

Rhodora! if the sages ask thee why
This charm is wasted on the earth and sky,
Tell them, dear, that if eyes were made for seeing,
Then Beauty is its own excuse for being.

— Emerson

The frost performs its secret ministry,
Unhelped by any wind.

— Coleridge

A thing of beauty is a joy forever;
Its loveliness increases;
it will never pass into nothingness.

— Keats

To me every hour of the light and dark is a miracle,
Every cubic inch of space is a miracle.

— Whitman

A drop of water has the properties of the sea,
but cannot exhibit a storm.

— Emerson

Come forth into the light of things,
Let Nature be your teacher.

— Wordsworth

Just after the death of the flowers,
And before they are buried in snow,
There comes a festival season
When Nature is all aglow.

— *Indian Summer*
1860, Author Unknown

That the yielding conquers the resistant
and the soft conquers the hard
is a fact known by all men,
yet utilized by none . . .

— Lao Tzu, 5th Century B.C.

Love all God's creation, the whole and every
grain of sand in it. Love every leaf, every ray of
God's light. Love the animals, love the plants,
love everything. If you love everything, you will
perceive the divine mystery in things. Once you
perceive it, you will begin to comprehend it better
every day. And you will come at last to love the whole
world with an all-embracing love.

— Dostoyevsky

We know each other very well.
We are all discerners of spirits.
Love, and you shall be loved.
Everything is superficial and perishes,
but love and truth only.

— Emerson

The daisy by the shadow that it casts,
Protects the lingering dewdrop from the sun.

— Wordsworth

Living Nature, not dull Art
Shall plan my ways and rule my heart.

— Cardinal Newman

Come see the north wind's masonry,
the frolic architecture of the snow.

— Emerson

. . . into the purple sea
The orange hues of Heaven sank silently.

— Shelley

I went to the woods because I wished to live
deliberately, to front only the essential
facts of life and see if I could not learn
what it had to teach, and not, when I
came to die, discover that I had not lived.

— Thoreau